FAY WELDON

Fay Weldon was born in England, brought up in New Zealand and educated in Scotland. Though best known for novels such as *The Lives and Loves of a She-Devil* and *The Bulgari Connection*, she is also a playwright – indeed much of her initial work was in television and radio drama.

Her first short stage play, in the anthology *Mixed Doubles* written at the end of the sixties, is still regularly performed, as is *Action Replay*, a study of alternative endings. Her first full-length play, *Woodworm*, about a Nobel Prize-winner having trouble with her husband, went to Broadway, while her adaptation of *Jane Eyre* went to the West End, *Tess of the D'Urbervilles* and *A Doll's House* toured the UK, and *The Four Alice Bakers* was a success for the Birmingham Playhouse.

For television she has written, among others, a pilot episode of *Upstairs Downstairs* and a four-part dramatised history of the feminist movement, *Big Women*. Amongst many plays for radio, one of the most outstanding is *Queen Gertrude PLC*, which starred Vanessa Redgrave.

She was made a CBE in 2001 for services to literature and published an autobiographical memoir, *Auto Da Fay*, the following year.

Other Titles in this Series

Fay Weldon

from the novel by Gustave Flaubert

MADAME BOVARY
Breakfast with Emma

NICK HERN BOOKS
London
www.nickhernbooks.co.uk

A Nick Hern Book

Madame Bovary: Breakfast with Emma first published in Great Britain in 2003 as a paperback original by Nick Hern Books Ltd.,
14 Larden Road, London W3 7ST

Madame Bovary: Breakfast with Emma copyright © 2003 by Fay Weldon

Fay Weldon has asserted her moral right to be identified as the author of this work

Front cover photograph: Mark Pennington

Typeset by Country Setting, Kingsdown, Kent CT14 8ES
Printed and bound in Great Britain by Bookmarque, Croydon, Surrey

A CIP catalogue record for this book is available from the British Library

ISBN 1 85459 775 2

Madame Bovary: Breakfast with Emma was first performed by Shared Experience Theatre Company at the Oxford Playhouse on 25 September 2003 and subsequently at Theatre Royal Bath; The Lowry, Salford Quays; Yvonne Arnaud Theatre, Guildford: Liverpool Playhouse; and the Lyric Hammersmith, London. The cast was as follows:

MADAME BOVARY	Amanda Drew
LHEREUX / LESTIBOUDOIS	Maxwell Hutcheon
FELICITE / MOTHER	Joanna Scanlan
CHARLES	Adrian Schiller
LEON / RODOLPHE	Simon Thorp

All other parts played by members of the company

Director   Polly Teale
Designer   Jonathan Fensom
Movement Director   Liz Ranken
Composer   Howard Davidson
Lighting   Chris Davey

ACT ONE

The breakfast room of Dr Bovary in the town of Tostes,
Northern France, in the 1850s.

Heavily furnished, respectable, bourgeois, but lightened by
Madame Bovary's pretty little frills, bows and knick-knacks.
It's early morning. The maid, FELICITE, is coming and going,
laying the breakfast table. FELICITE is thirtyish, cheerful,
businesslike, tart, self-interested. An ornate clock stands at
8.00.

FELICITE. Bread, freshly baked. Butter, freshly churned.
Madame's favourite confiture: apricot. Stand the coffee by
the fire to keep it hot. Milk, not so close it burns:
yesterday's milk, but Madame won't notice that for all she's
so particular. The waste in this household. Poor Monsieur.

A bang at the door, but it opens before she can get there.
It's an elderly villager, LESTIBOUDOIS, who serves as
everything from gravedigger to postman. He has a clutch of
letters. He adores FELICITE: she's impatient with him.

Here he comes again. The great black crow.

LESTIBOUDOIS. Why do you call me that? I don't like it.

FELICITE. Because when I open the door you blot out the
sunlight. You're a bird of evil omen. Mr. Lestoboudois.
What do you ever bring this household but bills and more
bills.

LESTIBOUDOIS. I don't know what's inside the envelopes,
and nor should you, Mademoiselle. It's not your business.
You're the servant. You'll get yourself into trouble. You
need a man to guide you. An older man, a man who's been
about, who knows the world.

FELICITE *snatches the letters.*

FELICITE. Oh, give those to me and get back to digging graves.

LESTIBOUDOIS. Someone has to dig the graves. It's a respectable and skilled occupation.

But the door is slammed in his face even as EMMA *swift and pretty comes running down the stairs in her morning gown to snatch the letters for herself. She flicks through them, wails at what she sees, removes a couple, gives the rest back to* FELICITE –

FELICITE. Madame –

But Madame whisks upstairs again: the door closes behind her –

(*To thin air.*) Madame can't keep her secrets for ever, for all she thinks she can. Monsieur will find out. Monsieurs always do, in my experience.

FELICITE *picks up a spoon* EMMA *has spun to the floor in her passing; she inspects it.*

Why must Madame have real silver? You can get plate for half the price, and it doesn't have to be polished all the time.

The door pushes open. LESTIBOUDOIS *again.*

The crow's back.

LESTIBOUDOIS. It upsets me when you call me that. I am not a stone, Félicité. I have feelings, like anyone else.

FELICITE. But what have they to do with me? What is the matter now?

LESTIBOUDOIS. The coachman's waiting at the Inn. He can't go on drinking coffee for ever. The little mistress must come this minute.

FELICITE (*yelling*). Berthe! Aren't you ready yet? (*To* LESTIBOUDOIS.) – The coachman's early: I won't have it said that Berthe's late.

A SMALL GIRL *now appears at the top of the stairs, dragging her suitcase. She's a plain child.*

LESTIBOUDOIS *goes to help her.*

She can carry it herself. She's strong enough.

LESTIBOUDOIS *desists, obediently. Berthe takes offence.*

Try and look more cheerful, child. You're going to your grandfather's, not a funeral.

BERTHE. I went to say goodbye to Mama and Papa, as I'm supposed, but their bedroom door was closed.

FELICITE. Your father was out on a call last night. I expect he's tired. A poor woman with pleurisy. She died in spite of all his efforts. That man is a saint.

BERTHE. I heard him go out, and I waited and waited and then I heard him come in.

FELICITE. You had no business being awake.

BERTHE. Well, I was. I was thinking of how I had to get up in the morning and travel all on my own.

FELICITE. You're quite old enough to travel alone, Berthe, and you like staying with your grandfather, you know you do. Stop feeling sorry for yourself.

BERTHE. But Mama won't even get up to say goodbye.

FELICITE. I'm here to say goodbye, isn't that good enough for you? And Monsieur here has come to take you to the coach so what's the matter with you? You're a very lucky little girl.

BERTHE. But he's the gravedigger, and he only comes for me because he likes you. No one likes me. I'm not pretty enough for Mama, and as for Papa, that's hopeless, he only cares about her.

FELICITE. That's enough of that, Berthe. Dear Lord, save me from children. And if I ever have one let it be a boy. Girls twist everything in their heads.

LESTIBOUDOIS. You will make a wonderful mother.

FELICITE. Do you think I want a fledging by an old back crow? It doesn't bear thinking about.

BERTHE (*going with* LESTIBOUDOIS). And Grandfather only puts up with me because I'm the only family he has and Mama will never go and visit him. I'm too small to travel alone. And take my bag, gravedigger. I can't carry it myself. It's too big.

FELICITE (*closing the door after them*). She's quite right. She is too young and her mother should have got up. Madam Bovary thinks only of herself. As does the daughter. As do I. As do all of us. If they don't come down soon, the selfish pigs, I suppose I'll have to make fresh coffee. More waste.

Stage goes dark. The title sequence over now, the real action begins. The clock begins to move on from eight o'clock. CHARLES, a good-looking, if unexciting country doctor sits opening letters at the breakfast table. He seems a little perplexed, as if expecting something that isn't there. EMMA comes downstairs, pretty in her morning gown, settles herself opposite CHARLES.

CHARLES. Emma –

EMMA. What is it, Charles?

CHARLES. I met Mr Lheureux in the street yesterday. He seemed cool towards me. Almost hostile.

EMMA. My dear, does one care when the draper is cool?

CHARLES. It is always pleasant to be liked.

EMMA. By the draper? Perhaps you'd like him to embrace you in public? You are the doctor: he is Lheureux, the draper. A shopkeeper.

CHARLES. He makes more money than I do, or ever will.

EMMA. Even in a village like this, there's such a thing as social distinctions. They need to be kept.

CHARLES. It's not a village, it is a town.

EMMA. It's a dull, dusty, small, boring village in a flat landscape which gets too much sun.

CHARLES. People live and die in it, my dear, however we describe it, and need a doctor.

EMMA. Someone has to do it, you mean.

CHARLES. Yes.

EMMA. You're a good man, Charles. No one has ever denied that.

CHARLES. I try to be.

She smiles; she cannot stay uncharming for long. He basks in her smile. He loves her.

Your cheeks are flushed. Are you well?

EMMA. Perfectly.

CHARLES. You're nervy. You're not going to be ill?

EMMA. No. Not ill.

CHARLES. Monsieur Lheureux said he'd put a letter in the post to me; There's nothing here, what can have happened to it?

EMMA. A letter? Shopkeepers don't send letters they send bills. Perhaps you misheard him.

CHARLES opens another letter.

CHARLES. But this is most certainly a bill, Emma. It's from the lending library. I don't believe this – it goes back three years. It's been left unpaid all that time. They want 15 hundred francs.

EMMA. There must be some muddle. They get nothing right. I suppose I do read a great deal. But what else is there to do, in a village? And I have to have the magazines to know what's going on. I have to keep up with the reviews, I must know what to wear. You would hardly want me to be dull, Charles, you know you would hate it. Now smile and be pleasant, please.

CHARLES. And for yet another day, there are no cheques, no bank notes, nothing came in. Nothing.

EMMA. People take a long time paying at this time of year. The harvest was bad, that never helps. God punishes us for our sins, according to Father Bournisien, though Monsieur Homais will have none of it: he says the reasons are scientific, and more to do with fertiliser than God's disapproval. What do you think, Charles?

CHARLES. Monsieur Bournisien is a priest and our friend Homais is a scientist, so obviously they will think differently.

EMMA. But what do you think, Charles? You are so very balanced in your view.

CHARLES. Now you want me to talk about God? When I am faced with a bill for fifteen hundred francs?

EMMA. What better time? The world is so wonderful and extraordinary a place, the sin is to lose sight of it. This morning's bread is so fresh and fine. We do have an excellent baker here in Yonville, Let us be grateful for that. You get on with healing the sick and looking after the poor and I will look after domestic matters, such as making sure the bread is fit to eat and paying the bills and I am sure we will continue very happily. We love one another, after all.

CHARLES. That goes without saying.

EMMA. Yes. Too often it does.

CHARLES. I am the man I am, Emma. Where's Berthe? Won't she be late for school?

EMMA. Berthe is already up and gone. She left for my father's on the early coach. She's to spend the next week or so at the farm. I thought she looked a little pale: a change of air will be good for her. I did mention it to you.

CHARLES. I don't recall it. She didn't say goodbye.

EMMA. We didn't want to wake you, Charles. You had such a disturbed night, you poor man.

CHARLES. The place feels empty without her. I knew something was wrong. You and little Berthe are what I work and live for, Emma. I am not a demonstrative man; I know that's considered a failing by a wife, but the only reason

I put up with the emetics, the leeches, the boils and pustules, the pus and the stench of gangrene, is for my family's sake –

EMMA. Charles, talk of anything: of life and death, of blessing and tragedy, of fatal illness and miraculous recoveries, but not, please, of pus, pustules and gangrene. Who wants such details over breakfast?

CHARLES. It's strange – if Monsieur Lheureux wrote me a letter, as he says he has, why isn't it here on the breakfast table? I do so hate unfinished business.

EMMA. Perhaps it fell through Monsieur Lestiboudois' fingers. He's better at digging graves than delivering letters. He shakes so.

CHARLES. Perhaps.

EMMA. You know he's in love with Félicité? Does the milk taste burned to you? Félicité keeps putting it too near the fire. I shall encourage her to be nice to the gravedigger: then she'll leave of her own accord and I won't have to fire her. That girl is so careless.

CHARLES. You are lucky to have a maid.

EMMA. What can you mean?

CHARLES. There are many women who do without servants altogether.

EMMA. But hardly your wife, Charles.

CHARLES. No, hardly my wife. I want you to be happy. There is a clear link between prosperity and happiness. Having maids and buying knick-knacks make women happy, or at least keeps them not unhappy. Being happy keeps them healthy. Had my wretched patient last night had firewood and food, she would not have died. She was too cold and hungry to survive: her husband's love was great but neither fed her nor warmed her sufficiently. Lord, how he cried when I told him she was dead.

EMMA. Would you miss me very much if I died, Charles?

CHARLES. What a strange question to ask.

EMMA. Would you?

CHARLES. I would be destroyed. Don't talk about it. It's unlucky.

EMMA. You recovered very quickly after your first wife died. Indeed, you came courting me before anyone knew she was even ill.

CHARLES. I was not courting you. I was visiting your father who had a broken leg.

EMMA. As if the more often you came the quicker the bone would mend. Oh yes.

CHARLES. It's true I loved you from the first moment I set eyes on you.

EMMA. You'd set eyes on someone else soon enough, I think, if I was not in the world, and love her just as well and just as much as me. Indeed, for all I know the poor woman who died last night has a beautiful daughter, and then I will pine and die just as your poor first wife did. I feel very much to blame for that, even if you don't.

CHARLES. It was an early marriage. She was much older then me. It was a mistake. It didn't count. And if you died, Berthe would certainly be destroyed. And I would be in no state to look after her: therefore, you are not allowed to die. You have to live. I will have a little more coffee. Even though, as you say, the milk does make it taste a little burned.

EMMA. My father loves Berthe. He'd be there to do the looking after.

CHARLES. Why are you talking like this? It's morbid.

EMMA. Yes, I expect it is. Take more jam with your bread, my dear. Don't you think there is something wonderful about apricots? They contain the sun: not just the heat and exhaustion of afternoon but the soft and rosy tenderness of evening.

CHARLES. I'm a dull old stick and not good enough for you. To me an apricot's just an apricot.

EMMA. It's the other way round. I am not good enough for you.

CHARLES *considers this a little.*

CHARLES. I think you've done something you're ashamed of, and that's what's the matter with you. You did get up to say goodbye to Berthe –

EMMA. Of course.

CHARLES. You should be closer to her. You yourself worry that you're not.

EMMA. Yes. That too.

CHARLES. To be sent off on her own like that – poor little girl . . .

EMMA. She's old enough to do without me. Indeed, she's better off without me.

CHARLES. Why do you say that? What's the matter with you, Emma? What are you hiding? I know you too well.

EMMA. I don't think you do. Indeed, Charles, you notice very little.

CHARLES. The truth is you didn't say goodbye to Berthe. You couldn't be bothered to get out of your bed to say goodbye to your own child: you were too comfortable where you were.

EMMA. I was not in bed, Charles.

CHARLES. We will get to the bottom of it, for your sake. (*Calling.*) Félicité!

EMMA. Charles, Félicité is the servant. You can't use her in evidence against me.

FELICITE (*appearing*). Monsieur?

CHARLES. Little Berthe got off all right this morning?

FELICITE *judges the situation and comes down on* EMMA'*s side.*

FELICITE. Oh yes, Sir. And Madame waved her goodbye and she went off smiling. She'll be happy enough with her grandfather, just for the week. She protests, but once she's there she settles nicely, to all accounts.

EMMA. That will be all, Félicité. Oh, but the milk. It doesn't taste right. I hope it is this morning's? It is either gone off or you burned it again.

FELICITE. Oh yes, Madam, it's fresh today. And I kept it well away from the fire.

EMMA. I am not sure I believe you, Félicité, but what can I do.

FELICITE, *betrayed, turns and goes, leaving* EMMA *wounded by her husband.*

You shouldn't have done that.

CHARLES. If it isn't Berthe, then it's something else. We'll get to the bottom of it. It will be trivial enough, I daresay. If you haven't even been paying your library dues, then what have you been doing with the money I give you? You're such a spendthrift.

EMMA. Perhaps you shouldn't have married me in the first place if you find me so unsatisfactory. Your mother warned you. You should have listened to her.

CHARLES'S MOTHER *comes in, agitated and elderly. The clock stops when others erupt into the breakfast scene, starts again when they depart.*

CHARLES'S MOTHER. Emma Bovary? The farmer's daughter? You can't possibly. Too young, too pretty, and too fanciful.

CHARLES. She will learn.

CHARLES'S MOTHER. But she will not. How can she? The girl grew up without a mother, poor thing. Her father is a peasant. She was sent to a convent school, for some reason. Her head will be stuffed with silly ideas. She has no idea what it is to be a wife or run a household.

CHARLES. She is enchanting.

CHARLES'S MOTHER. I can see that well enough. She will spend your money on fripperies. She will be cheated by the butcher. She will play the piano all morning and sleep all afternoon.

CHARLES. How can you know that?

CHARLES'S MOTHER. I have seen her finger-nails. They are too long. She does not understand hard work.

CHARLES. You do not want me to be happy.

CHARLES'S MOTHER. I do not want you to be unhappy, Charles.

CHARLES. My future lies with Emma. I proposed yesterday afternoon, and she accepted me. She knows she is inexperienced. She knows she has a lot to learn. But I believe she loves me. (*To* EMMA.) You did love me?

EMMA. Of course.

CHARLES. I have never regretted it. Never for one instant. I never expected you to be a perfect house wife, and you never were. But you are the brightness in my life. Without you, I am a dull old stick. I know you have done something you don't want to tell me, some little thing. Tell me and I'll forgive you. My pretty, darling, enchanting little Emma.

EMMA. You believe that if a woman feels something or does something, it is automatically little. That she has only tiny thoughts, fleeting passions.

CHARLES. It's true. Female passions are on a smaller scale than those of men. Last night when that poor woman passed away, her husband was utterly distraught, useless, he knew he had no future. Had it been he who died, the wife would have pulled herself together within minutes. I've watched by the bed while a man died, and five minutes later the woman was on her feet cooking as if nothing had happened.

EMMA. Because her children were hungry and she had no choice.

CHARLES. Well, yes, perhaps. Some of it will be necessity. Not all. Women are not given to despair, as men are. They're easily diverted.

EMMA. For many women, to have feelings at all is a luxury.

CHARLES. You are changing the subject, Emma, you are trying to divert me. But because I'm a man, it's not going to work. Come along now, sweetheart, are there other bills you haven't told me about? Is that it? Well, I daresay a woman must have a hat and a pair of shoes, even when her husband is a struggling country doctor with a batch of patients famous for not paying their fees.

EMMA. I do what I can. I organise your practice and do it very well. I write to your patients time and time again, asking them for the money they owe us. I badger them. It's not my fault if they don't pay up. The problem is you treat people who have no money.

CHARLES. Emma, a thought occurs to me. Last time you ran up debts with Mr Lheureux, and we had to sell the cottage to pay them off, I gave you power of attorney to deal with these matters. You did pay him what we owed him?

EMMA. Of course.

CHARLES. And you paid him in full?

EMMA. Stop lecturing me Charles. I am a grown woman. What is more, I have developed a very good business sense. Mr. Lheureux himself said so. Better perhaps than yours.

Enter Mr. LHEUREUX, carrying bales of black fabric, throwing them out for EMMA's inspection.

LHEUREUX. Madame Bovary, I bring you my most sincere condolences on the death of your husband's father. If you will forgive me saying so, your stature in this community of ours is even more significant than ever. Your style and beauty is what lends us grace: I cannot help noticing that your mourning shawl is a little worn. I have taken the liberty of bringing you this fine new barrege from Lyon – it is expected of you – as the one we all look up to. As to the matter of payment, you need only ask your husband to sign over power of attorney to you, it is commonly done – and there is no further need to bother him. Very often in a married couple it is the wife who has the best head for business. I would be honoured to bring the scarlet barrege over, too, Madame Bovary; if you would care to inspect that too. I should come to you, not you to me.

EMMA. I hope it's not very expensive.

LHEUREUX. You should see this fabric in scarlet. It suits the weave so very well.

EMMA. Oh yes, please, Mr. Lheureux. Before the day's out.

LHEUREUX, *well satisfied, whisks his merchandise away. The clock starts again.*

CHARLES. I daresay your business sense is indeed better than mine, Emma, you seem to know more about mortgages and leases and bills of credit than I do, but I know people, and I know the draper is not a man of principle. He dangles his wares in front of women, and if they are weak, if they are frivolous, they fall into temptation. Emma, promise me his letter is going to be about some new range of pipe cleaners and not money we owe him and I'll stop worrying.

EMMA. But of course it will be, Charles. Something little.

CHARLES. When he passed me in the street yesterday, he did not meet my eye.

EMMA. Because he did not see you, Charles. Poor Charles, you have your mother's disposition. Always so anxious about money. It was unbearable. The simplest thing an extravagance. Running to you behind my back.

CHARLES'S MOTHER. Charles, last night the candelabra was used yet again.

CHARLES. It casts such a lovely light. Emma loves to make the house pretty.

CHARLES'S MOTHER. There is no escaping that. But candles burn fast and cost money. Do you notice nothing?

CHARLES. Notice what?

CHARLES'S MOTHER. Everywhere I look there is some small extravagance. The milk must be thrown out every day. The laundry soap is scented. Shoes end up in the dustbin. Has she not heard of the menders? It is terrifying.

CHARLES. Mother, you must not be like this. This is Emma's home. She runs it in her own way.

CHARLES'S MOTHER. She does not run it at all. It just happens. And why do you always take her part? I scrimped and saved to get you through medical school and now I am not even welcome in my own home.

CHARLES. Mother, of course you are.

CHARLES'S MOTHER. Ever since I came here, every comment has been taken as a criticism, every piece of good advice brushed aside. But I won't trouble you any more.

CHARLES. Mother please, if I have offended you in any way – (*She crumples into her son's arms.*) – I will speak to Emma – of course I will.

EMMA. Your mother caused trouble from the beginning. She was impossible.

CHARLES. My duty was to her, my love and loyalty always to you. It was difficult for me.

EMMA. Oh, you should never have brought me to this miserable town in the first place. You can't take two steps without someone wanting to know your business. You can't light a candle without someone nagging about the cost –

CHARLES. But is was you who wanted us to move to Yonville. You said how you loved the softness of the air. And when we first came here you seemed so happy. That young student, what was his name –

EMMA. I don't know. It was a long time ago.

CHARLES. Léon, that was it– you seemed to have so much to say to him, that day we first arrived. And we met Mr Homais the chemist, who was to be so important in our lives. We all ate supper at the inn, remember, straight off the coach: a new life beginning for us, everything so fresh, everyone so full of ideas–

EMMA (*disparaging*). Mr. Homais! A chemist! He was certainly full of facts, though I would hardly say ideas.

Mr. HOMAIS drones on

MR. HOMAIS. Of course you will find the dwellings of our peasantry unhygienic in extreme. Enteritis, bilious attacks, marsh fever – not uncommon. The climate is not too bad – we even manage a few nonegenerians. The barometer drops

as low as four degrees in the winter and in high summer,
touches twenty five; thirty at the very most, which gives
us a maximum of seventy four Fahrenheit on the English
scale, no more. The state of the roads permits the use of a
cabriolet, so you are not doomed to a horse, and in general
the fees are quite healthy, the farmers being well off.
The considerable presence of cattle in the meadows which
exhale ammonia, that is to say nitrogen, hydrogen and
oxygen – no, just nitrogen and hydrogen and which sucks
up humus from the soil and combining with the electricity
circulating in the atmosphere, does engender some insalu-
brious miasmas – but by and large an intemperate heat is
cooled by south-easterly winds – Oh yes, our Yonville is a
fine place.

EMMA *is showing off her ankles, toasting her toes.*

EMMA. But are there any walks in the neighbourhood?

LEON. Hardly any. There is a spot they call the Pasture.
Sometimes on a Sunday I go and stay there with a book, to
watch the setting of the sun.

EMMA. A book is a great comfort.

LEON. It is indeed. I love to read.

EMMA. Me too. And the sunset can be a great inspiration.
Especially by the sea, they say.

LEON. Or indeed, sunset in the mountains. Who was the
musician who went to the mountains to excite his
imagination the more?

EMMA. I will remember his name in a minute. Are you a
musician?

LEON. No, but I love music.

EMMA. Me too.

CHARLES. A fanciful young fellow, as I remember. He talked
a lot about the soul. And he lodged with Mr. Homais, didn't
he, who being a rationalist, prides himself on having none.
Then he left for Paris to be a lawyer. We met up with him
once again, when we went to the opera in Rouen. Do you
remember that?

EMMA. I remember the opera, of course I do, we go so rarely.

CHARLES. You had so much to talk about, you and young
Léon, I'd felt quite left out. Not just sunset and mountains,
but art, poetry, music: debates I wouldn't dare enter into, for
all you were little more than a girl and I was the
knowledgeable man. You read so much, always off at the
library: your head full of fictions and fancies: it wasn't good
for you. I don't think you can have altogether forgotten him.

EMMA. I was pregnant, Charles – when we came to Yonville,
I was pregnant.

CHARLES. Forgive me.

EMMA. Good Lord, a woman can't be kept apart from male
company altogether, just because she got married. Charles,
really! I wouldn't have forgotten him, this young Léon, if
there had been more to it than was apparent, now would I!

CHARLES. I was not suggesting – Good God – never for a
minute –

Embarrassed, he rings the bell for FELICITE, *who bounces
in, none too pleased.*

FELICITE. Well, sir? What now?

CHARLES. Is there anyone in the surgery? Should I be there,
not here?

FELICITE. Nary a patient, sir. These days if they want
treatment, they go to the pharmacist. They go to Monsieur
Homais, which is against the law. They are meant to come
to you –

CHARLES. Monsieur Homais is a good fellow. A man of
science and very knowledgeable, Félicité. Pray don't worry
on my account.

FELICITE. So long as it don't affect my wages, anyone can do
as they want.

EMMA. Félicité, bring us more coffee, and this time make it
stronger: this is horribly weak.

FELICITE. We're almost out of coffee again, Madame, and I'll
not be the one to go scrounging round the town for more,

without the money to pay for it. What we have must last till next week.

EMMA. Don't answer back. I will not drink weak coffee. Make it properly as I've taught you. And do it now, this minute.

FELICITE *goes.*

Good coffee is one of life's pleasures, God given. I would rather be dead than go without.

CHARLES. Emma, what is the matter? That's a shameful thing to say.

EMMA. Being alive can be a very wearing and exhausting thing –

CHARLES. One can hardly not be alive at will.

EMMA. Well, one could. One could put an end to it.

CHARLES. One would have to have the means to do it.

EMMA. Oh, one has.

CHARLES. How? Where?

EMMA. Mr Homais keeps a store of arsenic in this house; in our cellar, where it's cool. His own cellar is so full, he uses ours as an overflow. Arsenic looks just like sugar: it could so easily be mistaken for it.

CHARLES. You've actually looked?

EMMA. Well, one has a certain fascination –

CHARLES. You didn't touch it? Even on the fingers . . . The stuff shouldn't be kept here. It isn't safe. Berthe, some servant, some innocent – mistakes happen so easily –

EMMA. It's properly labelled and sealed – don't upset yourself over nothing.

CHARLES. Well, if it obliges Mr Homais. He is our friend.

EMMA. Yes, indeed, our friend. We must not put Mr Homais, who knows everything, who is the wisest and most rational man in the world, who does not believe in God, who takes all our patients away so we are always in debt, to any inconvenience whatsoever.

CHARLES. I do not understand the edge in your voice.

EMMA. I'm sorry. Mr Homais is indeed our friend: he talks to you and is kind to me. I bear it in mind.

CHARLES. All the same, I will ask him to keep his own arsenic in his own cellar. He must make room for it somehow.

EMMA. I could still get hold of it, even if it was not in our cellar.

CHARLES. How would you do that?

EMMA. I could ask his servant to give it to me. Justin would do that. He'd do anything for me. He adores me: that's no secret, everyone knows.

CHARLES. The more reason for him not to give you a supply of arsenic for the asking.

EMMA. I would knock on the pharmacy door when Mr Homais was out. I would ask Justin for the key to the poisons cupboard. He would be astonished, but I would be so majestic, like some ghostly apparition – that though he would know in his heart something terrible was about to happen, still he could refuse me nothing! I would say, in any case, I only wanted poison to kill the rats which kept waking me up in the night. I would go straight to the shelf, seize the blue jar, tear out the cork, plunge in my hand, withdraw it full of white powder, and stuff it into my mouth. Justin would cry stop and throw himself upon me but it would be too late – too late –

CHARLES. Emma, you have worked all this out in your head.

EMMA. Yes. What else is there to do?

CHARLES. But you wouldn't ever do it –

EMMA. How can I tell – I feel one thing one day and another the next.

CHARLES. Emma, you would never want to do it –

EMMA. I could rise from this table, this moment, and do it.

CHARLES. It is wicked to even think these things. A sin against God.

EMMA. Then I am wicked. I am incorrigible.

CHARLES. No, you are not. You are simply silly. You have everything a woman could want. You have me for a husband. I love you with all my heart. Stop this stupidity. It is too upsetting.

EMMA. What has your love for me to do with anything?

CHARLES. The love of men is what women want.

EMMA. Yes, but there is love and love, Charles.

CHARLES. No. I think there is only one kind.

EMMA. But then you are a man. Oh, the mystery of women. Perhaps I am noble and want to save you from me, had you thought of that?

CHARLES. Today is a day like any other; but you are bored, nothing will do but you must stir things up and upset us all for the sake of it. I hate it when you're like this.

EMMA. I feel like a child learning to walk – it begins to run, it didn't mean to in the first place, but now it can't stop; it must run and run 'til it falls flat on its face. It must happen, it does happen: the tripping up, the sudden stop. I am not stirring things up on purpose, Charles, it's just perhaps the time has come. This is the day.

CHARLES. What are you saying now? What day?

EMMA. Only in retrospect could one say, that was the day: and then one would be dead and wouldn't know one had been right. How strange.

CHARLES. You're acting again. Why do you even think of death?

EMMA. I've told you why.

CHARLES. No, you've talked silliness, female hysteria. Look around you, Emma. Here you have the home you have made for us, pretty and charming, a husband who loves you, a child to give you meaning and future – good friends. What else is there for a woman to have in the world?

EMMA. Would it be enough for you?

CHARLES. But I'm a man. A man needs a purpose, something outside him. I heal the sick.

EMMA. I do love you, Charles. You are so innocent. I might indeed want to die to save you from me, though I thought at first I was only saying it.

CHARLES. What, save by dying? What fantasy is this?

EMMA. Jesus did it.

CHARLES. If Mr Homais is right about anything, it's in the dangers of a convent education. It puts sickly thoughts in a girl's head and they never go away. So, you would be crucified?

EMMA. I think that would hurt too much.

CHARLES. Yes. It would.

EMMA. You watch people die, Charles. What's it like? I imagine it to be a little thing. One would first fall asleep and it would all be over.

CHARLES. For most people death is a shame and a humiliation, grotesque, ugly, disgusting, painful and lingering. For those that remain behind it's worse. They must carry with them forever a vision of the one they loved, not in the fullness of health but in the pangs of death, disease and despair.

EMMA. It wouldn't be like that for me. Death would be quick and simple. Beautiful.

CHARLES. Why should it be different for you?

EMMA. I was never ugly in life, why should I be in death?

CHARLES. If you stuffed handfuls of arsenic in your mouth the way you describe you would end up very ugly indeed.

EMMA. You are just trying to frighten me.

CHARLES. No. I'm speaking the truth. I am glad Berthe isn't here to overhear her mother's latest silliness.

EMMA. I sent her away to make sure she would not. I had a feeling this might be the day. How can it be wicked to end a wicked life?

CHARLES *laughs.*

CHARLES. Bluebeard led a wicked life. It is scarcely in Madame Bovary's province so to do. What to run up a bill or so; sleep in of a morning and forget to wave goodbye to your child.

EMMA. I did wave goodbye, from the window. She could have looked up. She didn't.

CHARLES. I am afraid that in wickedness you are simply not in a position to compete with Robspierre. You will have to put up with it, Emma.

EMMA. You don't know me.

CHARLES. I think I do. This has not been a pleasant breakfast for me. Has it then been planned? If you are suggesting you sent our child away on purpose, I suspect you are plotting something. What?

EMMA. Don't say 'our child' in that pompous way. Say 'Berthe'. I sent her away because I did not trust myself. I simply did not know what was to happen next.

CHARLES. You felt the vapours coming on.

EMMA. How you do diminish me.

CHARLES. So now you are getting angry. Well, that's better than morbid ravings.

EMMA. Charles, listen to me. You must listen to me. You are a doctor, you go amongst people, but still you don't seem to understand how wicked they are, how cruel they can be.

CHARLES. You're married to me, and I'm neither wicked nor cruel. My mother is not wicked or cruel. Nor is Berthe. For you this town is the world and the townspeople are your friends. So what are you talking about? Wickedness? Cruelty?

EMMA. Oh indeed, if I look inside my own home, I can say with truth, I don't deserve you, Charles.

CHARLES. And surely as a married woman you have no business looking outside your home. If you do, you will encounter coarseness and crudeness, and you will meet the world's censure, and yes indeed, that is cruel. But it is not wicked. I thought you learned your lesson at the ball: do you remember, the Marquis' ball at Vaubyessard?

EMMA. Every day that passes is a day that separates me from it, and I hate the day because of it.

And the back of the stage is filled by dancing lords and ladies: a trifle misty, being seen through EMMA*'s eye — all is grace, charm and merriment –* CHARLES *and* EMMA*'s conversation continues.*

CHARLES. We were asked out of pity.

EMMA. That is not true. They asked us because they saw in me something finer: they could not ask me without asking you; but you would dance; you made us a laughing stock–

CHARLES. One has the misfortune to be asked to a ball – what can a man do but dance about?

EMMA. They were lords and ladies – they were people of grace and distinction – I belonged with them –

CHARLES (*disparaging*). Oh yes, amongst pomegranates and pineapples, while the people go hungry –

EMMA. Mock all you like –

CHARLES. It isn't sensible to step outside one's station. It leads only to humiliation.

EMMA. The women were so fine, exquisite, so beautiful – their skin had such a lovely transparency, like porcelain: how is that done, Charles? How does it come about? The delicate complexion of the rich?

CHARLES. I have certainly heard Mr Homais say a well-ordered diet of exquisite food can affect the skin – it certainly affects the disposition to make it disagreeable. Or who's to say, it may be something they, well, choose to take, which then affects their whole constitution. But you would not know about that. They like to be over-excited, for all their apparent formality. There was a great deal of whispering behind fans, and oglings, and droppings of handkerchiefs and other indecent excitements – and you were a hit with that foolish fop, the Viscount, and it went to your head. I stood by the banister and waited for you, but you would dance on –

Enter the VISCOUNT *to waltz with* EMMA.

VISCOUNT. The countryside is so perfect for a weekend

EMMA. I so agree. Perfect!

VISCOUNT. How charmingly you dance. You have a real gift for it, an inner grace. Have I seen you before – at the Duc du Beauvais' place, perhaps?

EMMA. Perhaps.

VISCOUNT. Evidently. We must meet again in the season, in Paris. I will make very sure you have an invitation –

They dance into obscurity: EMMA *comes back to take off her slippers.*

EMMA. When finally I came to bed that night, you had gone to sleep.

CHARLES. I was exhausted.

EMMA. You often are, Charles.

CHARLES. I do a day's work, and often a night's as well.

EMMA. Do you remember the dress I wore?

CHARLES. No.

EMMA. Well, you wouldn't. But it was beautiful. It was a gown of pale saffron silk, trimmed with roses; I made it to a fashion plate I found in a magazine; I wore my hair in a chignon –

CHARLES. I remember you being beautiful. I don't remember what you wore. I was jealous because you danced with others. Well, I was younger then.

EMMA. I've loved the feel and look of saffron silk ever since. You say I was taught a lesson: we weren't asked again, the invitation to Paris never came, all that. But the lesson I learned was that just because you're a farmer's daughter and a doctor's wife doesn't mean you have to be dull and plain: if only you keep up you can be as good as anyone.

CHARLES. What do you mean, keep up?

EMMA. Follow the fashions, read the latest novels, know what art shows are successful, which restaurants one can be seen in – then if something like that happens again, I can hold a proper conversation. I can chatter away and charm with the best of them. And I do keep up, I do. I know the map of Paris by heart, Charles. All the avenues, the parks, the theatres –.

CHARLES. Emma, if so much as remembering a stupid ball fifteen years back can so distress you –

EMMA (*calling*). Félicité.

FELICITE *plonks down fresh coffee, which is ignored.*

FELICITE. What now?

EMMA. In tissue paper, in the little drawer of my closet, are a pair of dancing shoes. I need them now.

FELICITE. What for?

EMMA. Just fetch them.

FELICITE *shrugs and goes.*

CHARLES. I have known you like this once or twice before: you make yourself ill. Shall I call my mother – ?

EMMA. Oh no, no, no!

CHARLES. She understands more than you think.

EMMA. She understands about bodies. She is like you. She can prepare a poultice, bring down a fever. But hearts and souls? No. She thinks these are trivia.

CHARLES. She may know more than you think. You are not the only one to suffer.

EMMA. Your mother always said I was too excitable. She thought I would be the ruin of you. She was right.

CHARLES. Ruined? Me? A man in a secure position who enjoys the respect of the community I work in?

EMMA. Respect? You believe you are respected?

CHARLES. Yes indeed I do.

EMMA. Then why is there no one in your consulting room?

CHARLES. Thanks to my advice and treatment the townsfolk are a healthy lot. I remember my father telling me how strange the doctor's occupation was: the better he did his job the poorer he became. My dearest, we have a fulfilling life; we do our duty by others: I have never refused you anything: your drawers and closets are overflowing with fine things; your dressing table is a sea of trinkets –

EMMA. Trinkets! Oh Good Lord you would point at a statue of Napoleon and say what a fine horse, I like the way his tail flows.

CHARLES. Yes, and what would be wrong with that –

Enter FELICITE *with slippers* –

FELICITE. Are these the ones you mean?

EMMA. Yes.

CHARLES. Why have you kept a pair of old dancing shoes?

EMMA. They're the ones I wore the night of the ball. I have such little feet, almost like a doll's. I was born to dance, and look at me now! I will be well out of it all-.

CHARLES. Félicité, will you go –

FELICITE. When I opened Madam's closet a moth flew out. A clothes moth. There may have been more than one.

EMMA waits.

Is something the matter with Madam? It's not my fault the clothes moths have got in. Madame will not give me enough camphor. She doesn't like the smell. I am waiting for breakfast to be finished so I can clear the table and get on. It is customary for people to sit and chatter over dinner, I know, but these days its getting to be breakfast too. No one thinks about the servants.

EMMA. Go away, Félicité. Leave us alone –

FELICITE. But you keep calling me in.

EMMA. You are such a stupid girl. Go away.

FELICITE goes.

It is shaming to have to live with such people. They spoil the air one breathes. Charles, do you see the soles of these slippers?

CHARLES. You wore them out, that night.

EMMA. See how yellowed they are? That's from the sandalwood oil they put on the ballroom floor. Even the floors glowed. We have these rough and rustic planks

CHARLES. This is a good solid house, fitted to our position in the town.

EMMA. Something entered my soul that night, seeped into it, as my slippers took in the golden oil.

The VISCOUNT *appears, dancing on.*

CHARLES. Discontent, perhaps, because you weren't married to a Viscount? I think you did well enough marrying a doctor. You are a farmer's daughter, a pretty one, but all the same – these people marry their own. Anyway, you were already married, to me.

EMMA. Perhaps I was switched at birth. The wet nurse handed my mother the wrong baby. Put the slippers to your cheek, Charles, the scent still lingers. Long after I am gone, it will still be there.

CHARLES. It's a horrible carrion smell. You must not be flippant: you must not talk like this: you must not pretend to yourself like this, or it will begin to feel true. People who talk about suicide do it, whatever others may say to the contrary.

EMMA. Suicide! That's a harsh and bitter word –

CHARLES. It's what you are talking about.

EMMA. No. Suicide is a mortal sin.

CHARLES. Quite.

EMMA. I've been playing with the idea, that's all. As one niggles a bad tooth. I'll stop now. No more gloomy talk. I'm sorry.

CHARLES. Give me the slippers –

EMMA *does.*

EMMA. Don't, don't!

But CHARLES *throws them on the fire. She grovels after them, trying to rescue them. Cries out as she burns her hand –*

CHARLES. Now you've burnt yourself.

EMMA. Yes.

CHARLES. Then don't invite death. Curb your dramas, Emma.

EMMA. My lovely slippers. I kept them safe for so long. You're trying to destroy something in me. I know you are. You always have. All our marriage you've tried to kill my soul.

CHARLES. Oh flapdoodle.

EMMA. I don't care what Mr Homais says. We do have souls, and they can wither up and die, and then what use is the body?

CHARLES. Emma, I don't know whether to laugh or cry. Will you go back to bed? Start this day again?

EMMA. See, my hand is raw where the flames burned. It's your fault. Do you think hell is real?

CHARLES. Yes, of course.

EMMA. You say that to make me afraid to die. Of course it might be true. God might send me to hell. But I think when I was a convent girl I was made to say enough Hail Marys to earn some remission from the flames. I shall comfort myself with that.

CHARLES. Even at your worst you can make me smile. Why isn't it enough for you that I love you?

EMMA. How I cried and prayed at the foot of the cross. I was in love with death, with renunciation. I saw myself as the Virgin Mary. I wanted to be a bride of Christ. I need to confess to you, Charles. I think this is what it is about. I want to die in a state of grace.

CHARLES. Then fetch Father Bournisien: the sooner the better. You would not dare speak to him in this fashion. You would be ashamed.

EMMA. But you're the one I've sinned against. You're the one who must forgive me. God forgives easily enough, I am not sure husbands do.

Truth begins to dawn on CHARLES.

CHARLES. Wait, wait. What are you telling me?

EMMA. And do you know, when I went to them for help they refused me. They would have nothing to do with me.

CHARLES. They?

EMMA. I thought love meant something, I thought love saved the world and us poor wretches with it, but I was wrong. It vanishes. It goes. How can I go on living? There is nothing in here to be alive.

CHARLES. You have loved other men? During the course of our marriage?

EMMA. Yes. You think women have trivial emotions, little passions, I tell you they have more than that.

CHARLES. But you've loved them only in the head – in your imagination.

EMMA. What do you know about anything? You never have. These silly painted walls, this stupid solid table – nothing. The world of practical things, of debts and debtors and being frightened of Mr Lheureux – nothing.

CHARLES. This love you felt for other men – if I hear you right – was in the head. Anything else, anything more, is unthinkable. To even contemplate it is to feel disgust –

EMMA. What is all this shock about? Queens and Empresses do it all the time. It is expected of them. They marry as virgins, produce the necessary heirs, and then they get on with their real lives; lovers, wild emotion, beauty, laughter, passion – why should it not be the same for me? Except, oh Charles, the world has turned out to be such a disappointment.

CHARLES. This is fantasy. It must be.

EMMA. Why must it be? I am a woman. I am alive.

CHARLES. You are my wife.

EMMA. Oh Dr Bovary, good Dr Bovary, blind, deaf Dr
Bovary, you are only the same as half of the rest of the
world. Half of the world has unfaithful wives, and half the
husbands in it deserve them.

CHARLES. This is just stupid drama. You are making it up to
upset me.

EMMA. You must believe me or you can't forgive me, and
without your forgiveness I may indeed go to hell. Hell is
real, I have felt it.

CHARLES. Tell me who you are talking about. Give me a
name.

EMMA. Léon. The student.

CHARLES. Now I know you are lying. You were pregnant
when we knew him, when we first came to Yonville. It is
out of the question. Léon! I have heard from Homais of
women who have such fantasies – I found them revolting.
I don't know what to do. You must stop talking like this,
Emma. Please. I don't know what you're trying to do, or
why. You will destroy us.

EMMA. I am destroyed already. I want not to destroy you, for
some reason. The only way out is to speak the truth and die.

CHARLES. Oh stop it, stop it. You have managed to turn this
room, this familiar space, into a nightmare. No more words,
Emma. There is no unsaying them. They show me the
hidden places in your head.

EMMA. Is what is in my head so terrible?

CHARLES. Yes. I find it so.

EMMA. Sweet little Madame Bovary, who would have thought
what was going on inside her pretty little head. Well, now
they'll know. I'm going to do it, Charles. You threw my
slippers in the fire, as if they were worthless. If they are, so
am I. Better dead.

CHARLES. Have you worked yourself up to this out of nothing? It is beyond belief. Or has something happened you are not telling me? Yes, that's it, isn't it. Some terrible event has left you deranged. Tell me what happened, what was done to you, Emma. Whatever it was you will not be to blame, I promise not to hold it against you. You are so innocent.

EMMA. What happened? Nothing happened. I was in love with Léon. Léon was in love with me. We said nothing, we did nothing. A gesture here, a look there. A night made sleepless by desire. We met in the inn and we talked about books. It is lodged in my heart.

EMMA *toasts her toes: we are back when they met.*

LEON. What in the world is better than an evening by the fire, with the wind beating on the window panes, the lamp burning –

EMMA. Oh, yes –

LEON. Your head is free, the spirit roams, the hours slip away: from your chair you journey through the universe, you become one with your characters. It seems as if your own heart is beating under their skin.

EMMA. It is just like that – the world is suddenly so rich.

LEON. And when you read a passage that puts into words your deepest feelings – your inmost thoughts – when those you encounter in the world of the imagination are good, and noble, and full of courage–

EMMA. And the story touches the heart, and you find therein the echo of all that you knew without knowing – and you escape altogether the tedium of everyday life –

LEON. It is the same for me, Madame Bovary.

EMMA. I love the kind of story in which events press inexorably on to end in some great act of heroism which you can see coming – I hate it when the characters are commonplace, the way people are in life.

LEON. I think we are kindred spirits, you and I.

EMMA (*to* CHARLES). But what is the point if the kindred spirit is married, and virtuous? I was consumed by longing, Charles. You didn't notice. I became very thin and rather ill: he became bored and restless because nothing did happen, and there must be an end to unrequited love. He went to Paris to study law. That was all.

CHARLES. It is hard to live with, that your thoughts and your desires were with another man. Scarcely a man, a stripling, a student, a no-one. But you were young. I can forgive it. I have no choice.

EMMA. God gave us love, and a duty to feel it, to experience its joys.

CHARLES. You swear that was all? On the bible, swear it.

He takes the Bible and tries to hold her hand over it, but she won't.

EMMA. Later, though, we met him once again, quite by chance. Or perhaps it was destiny. He said it was. Or God's will, how otherwise could it happen? We went to the Opera in Rouen, do you remember?

CHARLES. Of course. It was midsummer. Very hot. I had worn too may clothes. And the plot was complicated.

EMMA (*as music builds*). It was beautiful. So beautiful and yet so sad.

They set up the opera box and sit in their seats.

Her voice echoed my voice, my thoughts were hers, my lamentations and my joy the same. The music flooded through me like a tide –

CHARLES. Yes, but what's happening? Why is she clutching her throat. Is she ill?

EMMA. Charles, that is her lover.

CHARLES. Even so! I can't hear the words for the music. I do need things to be made clear. What has he done to offend her?

EMMA. Oh please, hush.

CHARLES. No, tell me.

EMMA. Later, Charles, please.

CHARLES. But he is such an oaf. So much warbling and to what end? You'll never guess who I saw on the stairs just now, when we came in. Léon. Remember, the student? He said he'd join us at the interval, if I can endure this 'til then.

Enter LEON *just as the second act begins. He kisses* EMMA*'s hand and sits beside her. The singer sings a romantic song that echoes their plight.* EMMA *begins to sing and* LEON *responds. They have become the opera.* CHARLES *fans himself with his programme.*

The heat is too much. I'll see you outside. Léon will take care of you.

EMMA. Léon? How did you find me?

LEON. Coincidence, blind instinct. The moth to the flame. I felt you drawing me near.

EMMA. No, tell me the truth.

LEON. I sought you out. We have unfinished business Emma. You must know that. How have you been?

EMMA. Burdened by responsibilities of the dullest kind. And you?

LEON. Bored by the law, attracted by other vocations, harassed in letters by my mother who wants me to marry. Restless.

EMMA. Why restless?

LEON. Because the soul cries out for love, and there is no finding it, and no walking by the river and talking with a soul mate.

EMMA. If only you knew how I have dreamed.

LEON. After we parted, I came across an Italian print in an engraver's shop: was one of the Muses, draped in a tunic, gazing at the moon. I went there time and time again, just to look at it. I would stay hour after hour. When I looked at her, I saw you.

EMMA *gasps with the romance of it all.*

EMMA. Don't say it. We are brother and sister to each other. I'm too old, you are too young. I am married. You must go now.

LEON. Have mercy. Let me see you again. We have such important things to say to each other.

EMMA. No. We can't, mustn't.

LEON. Please.

EMMA. Tomorrow morning, at the Cathedral of Notre Dame. I am sure with Our Lady to look after us we will be safe from indiscretion.

The Cathedral bell chimes. EMMA *is at prayer.* LEON *enters. She stands to face him.*

No. I was wrong. It must not be. Everything I believe in, trust and honour – Charles . . . I cannot.

The verger pushes between them, silly old bore, and she follows him.

Over to the left please, to see where once the great bell of Amboise stood. It weighed fifty thousand pounds, and the workmen who cast it, died of joy, here in this very spot. Under this simple seat lies Pierre de Brèze, killed at the battle of Montlery in 1465. People take too little interest in history. Weeping, to his left, is Diane de Poitiers, born 1499, died 1516 and of special interest to the young ladies is the Blessed Virgin, child in her arms – don't stray from the group please –

LEON. Come with me, now –

EMMA. But the Cathedral is so beautiful.

LEON. You are so beautiful.

LEON. These are the magnificent Amboise tombs, cardinals and archbishops of Rouen. This one was an important minister, under Louis the Twelfth, said to be a perfect representation –

LEON. That is enough. Enough –

He steers her away and into a cab. They sit side by side.

EMMA. The two of us, alone in a cab? It's not the thing.

LEON. Everyone does it in Paris.

EMMA. It would be interesting to see Paris. The streets I had read about, traced with my fingers –

LEON. Get in! For God's sake drive –

He embraces her, she succumbs, she drops a torn-up letter from the window which the wind blows away – her voice continues – the horses speed up – they make love.

EMMA. Tried to imagine a thousand times –

LEON. Further, my man. Faster –

EMMA'S VOICE. The way I had memorised – La Grande Chaussée, Le Jardin des Plantes, Saint Séver, Le Quai de Curandiers, Le Quai aux Mentes, La Place du Champ de Mars – Saint Pol, Leseure, Mont Gagnon, Le Rouge Marc, La Place du Gaillardbois, La Rue Saint Maladrerie, La Rue Dinanderie –

EMMA. No, don't stop, don't stop!

They gasp in climax. The trotting of the horse slows, stops.

CHARLES. In a coach, like a whore?

EMMA. Like a woman in love.

ACT TWO

The hands of the clock are where we last saw them. CHARLES *and* EMMA *still sit at the table.*

EMMA. It was easy enough, Charles. A woman has to go here and there when she runs a household. She can go anywhere. Sometimes she does.

In spite of all, she is pleased with herself. CHARLES *is incredulous.*

CHARLES. You were a different person then. Younger. You wouldn't do it now.

EMMA. Only because I have lost my trust in love, my faith in men. Men aren't up to it. They don't have the staying power of women, or the courage. They like their pleasures, but they're weak: they can't see things through.

CHARLES. No. None of it's true. You just enjoy tormenting me. You wouldn't have dared deceive me.

EMMA. Charles, I would dare anything in love. I would risk everything. The worst thing that can happen is death, and death is not so bad a fate: simply to finish. You don't know me very well, do you? For all you say you love me, you were not very interested in me, or only as a possession.

CHARLES. I would rather not know you at all, if this is what there is to know.

EMMA. And I am to be pitied, as much as you.

CHARLES. Because you have had to live with your conscience? Pitied?

EMMA. No. I feel all kinds of things, but not the aggravation of a bad conscience.

CHARLES. You are unbelievable.

EMMA. I am truthful.

CHARLES. Then I don't want your truths.

EMMA. I was brought up to speak it, my dear. One is meant to.

CHARLES. That's a very strange way to address me, in the circumstances. My dear.

EMMA. But you are my dear. You've no idea the unhappiness I've felt.

CHARLES. It is your unhappiness, not mine. Why should I feel it for you?

EMMA. Because you married me. You took me on.

CHARLES. You are not entitled to the privileges of being a wife, since you won't take on its duties.

EMMA. Duties! So cold! I feel death already. Charles, you have to forgive me. I have to be shriven. You must!

CHARLES. Was it because he was so good-looking? Was that it? Younger than me? Taller? More interesting than me? Did he please you more?

EMMA. It was nothing to do with you.

CHARLES. Nothing to do with you either, it seems. You show no shame, no remorse, as if it was someone else doing these loathsome, whorish things.

EMMA. It was love. It seemed to me love was the highest thing. I have tried to explain it to you.

CHARLES. Duty, kindness, your feelings for your husband, your duty as a wife? All nothing?

EMMA. This was stronger.

CHARLES. Then you are no better than an animal.

EMMA. How can you say that? Animals don't feel as I do. It is because I can't feel love anymore I know I am better dead. There, you have it.

CHARLES. Who else?

EMMA. I don't understand you.

CHARLES. I said, who else? Who else have you fucked?

EMMA. Don't use that word.

CHARLES. It's what animals do, and the peasants you so despise. They fuck like animals. As you do.

EMMA. I don't want to speak to you if you are going to be so coarse. It wasn't like that. None of it was like that.

CHARLES. And who knows about this? Everyone? Who else knows your filthy habits? How many in the town know, and pity me? Well?

EMMA. Indeed, no one does. I have been so careful.

CHARLES. Does the maid know?

EMMA. Of course not.

CHARLES. Liar. It explains her contempt for you.

EMMA. She is loyal to me.

CHARLES. Then she does know.

EMMA. She came long after –

CHARLES. Long after what?

EMMA. Long after Léon had left me, had discarded me. Charles, I have only you now. You are my only friend. There is no one else. I am so alone. That's why I have to speak the truth to you.

CHARLES. Then there was someone else. Who?

EMMA. No one else.

CHARLES. Liar.

He is on his feet. So is she, in terror. He will shake it out of her if he has to kill her.

EMMA. Rodolphe.

CHARLES. Rodolphe? Rodolphe Boulanger? Impossible.

EMMA. Why impossible?

CHARLES. That brash, vulgar man. No. Not you. It's like your talk of death, a sickness and an attack on me. You choose the most unlikely, most distressing notion, and use it to upset. You talk about your wishes and your fantasies as if they were real. Rodolphe Boulanger! You entertain yourself and distress me with the fantasy of illicit love: you cannot live without the drama of it. Léon was possible, I can see that. But Rodolphe Boulanger, no.

EMMA. Why not?

CHARLES. It takes two. Why would he be interested in you? A little unsophisticated country doctor's wife He can have anyone, and indeed he's rumoured so to do. A revolting person, slick and greasy. I don't think even you would sink so low. His was just the first name to come into your poor deluded head.

EMMA. It went on for years. It was your fault.

CHARLES. Oh yes. How my fault?

EMMA. Because you are the man you are. Because compared to Rodolphe you are dull, slow-witted, clumsy and vulgar. Rodolphe is a man of the world. You are an oaf of a country doctor. He is a landowner, He is rich, a bachelor, stylish, fashionable: he owns property in the area. He is somebody!

CHARLES. You were pleased enough to marry me. What was your fate otherwise? To marry some country bumpkin with a few acres?

EMMA. You are a bumpkin of a doctor. Self-satisfied, without ambition, or proper income, or any style at all. When you are not complacent you are simply ridiculous. To be married to someone like you is a daily humiliation, a crucifixion. There she goes, they say, Madame Bovary: how they watch me: poor thing, they think, he can't get up to much. It's all he can do to get out of bed in the morning, let alone do anything but sleep when he gets into it. I cannot endure being pitied.

CHARLES. What they think when they look after you, Madame Bovary, is whore, slut, trollop. They deride you; no doubt they pity me. You have ruined me. I wish I had never set eyes on you. I believe you now. When you had finished with poor Léon the student, you fucked the odious Rodolphe Boulanger.

EMMA. That word again. The crudeness! What a pity you killed your first wife off. She must have suited you so much better than me, poor, miserable thing. How much older than you was she? Twenty years! I knew nothing when you married me, nothing. I did not know what was on offer in the world. You had no business marrying me and locking me up here, keeping me prisoner.

CHARLES. Believe me, you are free to leave.

EMMA. Where would I go?

CHARLES. Where indeed? Your lovers seem to know better than to carry you off. They take their pleasures and then off-load you back on to me.

EMMA. It wasn't like that.

CHARLES. No? Then why are you here, since I'm such a failure as a man and a husband?

EMMA. I have a child to think of.

CHARLES. I hadn't noticed it.

EMMA. She isn't a rewarding child. Not the one I hoped to have. She is a disappointment to me. She takes after you. How can I possibly love her?

CHARLES. Be careful what you say.

EMMA. You will all be sorry when I am dead.

CHARLES. That again. Up it comes, the refrain. Careful or I'll kill myself. It's horrible and pathetic.

EMMA. I mean it.

CHARLES. No. You mean to tell me about Rodolphe and entertain yourself by my pain. Do you charge for your favours? Is that where all the silks and fineries come from, the patchouli for your handkerchiefs, the bracelets round that evil little wrist, the rings on the wandering fingers and the necklaces that weigh down your soul? You live, come to think of it, like a whore. There's no way my earnings can afford us these things. They are gifts from your lovers.

EMMA. Men hate parting with cash. That at least has been my experience. They will offer gifts, gold and jewellery, in the first flush of adoration, but not money. Money is dangerous: it might offer her an independent means of escape. No, Charles, I was the one who gave, because I love to give. Because I wanted my lover to have something of me, to hold against his cheek in my absence, something rare and precious and special. In memory of delight that had been, in the expectation of more delight to come. Except too often there was none to come. Charles, I have been so disappointed, disappointed to the quick. I hurt. Pity me.

CHARLES. Who, me? Pity you? Me, the dull country doctor? The one you couldn't take anywhere? The clod-hopping oaf at the Marquis' ball? What use is my pity to you?

EMMA. I shouldn't have said those things. I'm sorry. You have been good to me, after your fashion. If I die it will be for your sake, because I'm no use to myself and you are better off without me.

CHARLES. In a cab, was it, with Rodolphe, or beneath a lamp post in the street, or up against some alley wall, skirt around your waist?

EMMA. It was at the Agricultural fair. We fell into conversation. That was all.

RODOLPHE *appears on stage, a fine vigorous macho figure of a man he is too. Very personable.*

RODOLPHE. Madame Bovary! In person! A delight to the eye, diminishing in glory the sun itself. It is a fine day for an Agricultural fair, is it not. Blue skies and birds twittering. Will you sit with me for a little, while we see who has ploughed the straightest row, who has grown the finest carrot.

EMMA. And who has prepared the longest speech.

RODOLPHE. Perhaps we should give our own prize, to the greatest bore.

EMMA. We will be spoilt for choice, I fear. If Monsieur Homais is to speak my betting is on him. He will never stop.

RODOLPHE. Well, we are doomed to live in the countryside, you and I, so we are doomed to live amongst clod hoppers.

Those who live their lives as if there were no greater joy than the sight of a well-fed pig in a clean sty.

ADJUDICATOR. Attention! The prize for marrows is shared by Monsieur Belot and Monsieur Cullembourg.

EMMA. They can't be blamed for their simplicity. They are good people, devoted to duty.

RODOLPHE. Duty! That shocking word. I never want to hear it again in my life. Our only human duty is to feel what is noble and cherish what is beautiful. All other duty is another word for respectability.

EMMA. But we can't all live our lives as we want. We must take notice of what others say and think.

ADJUDICATOR. Swine Category No 2, Cochon du Nouvel Monde, Monsieur Caron.

RODOLPHE. We must recognise morality, of course. But what kind? The sort that men have invented, that changes all the time, that brays with the mob? Or that other overarching one, inspiring, like the fields around us and the skies above us, that recognises greatness –

EMMA (*out of her depth*). Oh that one.

ADJUDICATOR. Prize for the best cultivation of hemp in the Commercial Division, Monsieur Bain of Givry-St-Martin. And to Catherine Leroux of Sassetot, for fifty four years service to the same farm, a silver medal. Where is the old dear? Is she deaf? Madame Leroux?

RODOLPHE. It is a social conspiracy, it is revolting, don't you agree? All emotions are undermined, all sympathies persecuted and maligned. If ever two pure souls should meet, their love would be destroyed before they even began.

EMMA. Excuse me – forgive me – my husband will be wondering where I am.

RODOLPHE. Of course. You must go. But you will come riding with me? Your husband agrees you need the air. Indeed it is his suggestion.

EMMA. Yes, of course. No. I am not sure. Charles, I tried to resist him, I knew where it would lead. I said I wouldn't go riding with him, I had no riding habit. You said I should get one made. I said I had no horse, you said you would buy me one. You pushed me into his arms.

CHARLES. I was concerned for your health.

EMMA. You acted like a buffoon. You said you could not afford to buy a horse. He offered to lend me one. I refused. You accepted. You drove me into his arms by being so stupid.

CHARLES. So this too is my fault?

EMMA. Yes.

CHARLES. If you refused him it was to be the more sure of him. Women's tricks. Where did you go riding? If I can see it my head, I might be better able to believe it.

EMMA. To the hills above Yonville. The day was so clear and bright. You could see for miles. I looked back and I could just make out this house, Charles. And you were there inside: the knowledge made me feel safe.

CHARLES. Even that didn't stop you? Knowing I trusted you, and thought no evil of you?

EMMA. How could you think any evil, being such a good man? We rode together towards the forest: the day was overcast; the ground overlaid with pine needles, even the sound of the hooves was softened. A carpet ready made for us, thick and soft. As we entered the forest, the sun came out.

RODOLPHE. I am too much in love. I think of you all the time. I see you at the corner of every street. Not to be with you breaks my heart. At night, every night, I get out of bed and leave my room, and gaze at your house. I watch as you close your door, draw the curtains, put out the light. You never knew that out in the darkness this pathetic creature suffered so.

EMMA. Please. Stop.

RODOLPHE. Forgive me. I offend you. I will go.

EMMA. Please stay.

RODOLPHE. One day you find her. Just when you have given up hope. When everything seems shallow, meaningless, absurd. You find her. The one who understands what makes you breathe, to whom all secrets can be told, all desires made known. You will give her everything you have, sacrifice every thing for her. Forgive me. (*They kiss.*)

CHARLES. I trusted you.

EMMA. I could not help myself.

CHARLES. Madame Bovary could not help herself –

EMMA. And although until that day his aim might have been seduction, afterwards it was not. It was love. That happens, you know. If you have indeed found the destined one.

CHARLES. Afterwards, he will have despised you. Men do.

EMMA. No. It was not like that.

CHARLES. When you came back from the ride, I told you how well you looked, which indeed you did, and I went out to buy you a horse, so you could go riding some more.

EMMA. An old horse, broken-winded, bought for a pittance. I was ashamed of it, and you for buying it.

CHARLES. Bitch!

EMMA. I will stop there if you want.

CHARLES. No. Go on.

EMMA. You were so often out, Charles, patching up the yokels, it was easy for us – we'd leave each other letters down by the river: secret places we arranged. We had lovers' luck: we rejoiced in it. If you left the house early in the morning, Charles, I'd pretend to be asleep, and slip out of the house as soon as you were gone, and take the horse, and ride by the empty back roads to Rodolphe's house, and slip into his bed while he still slept –

CHARLES *can hardly believe it.*

You should not have left me alone so much. You ignored my existence. I began to feel I had none. Bed to you was just for sleeping. Out of doors? Unthinkable. And I would weep when I had to leave him, my body still soft and marked by our lovemaking.

CHARLES. And then he got tired of you.

EMMA. How do you know? Because you are a man like any other? I hardly think so.

CHARLES. I have patients. Scum of the earth, many of them. I know what goes on.

RODOLPHE. Emma, are you ill? Why are you crying?

EMMA. Because I always have to leave you. I don't want to go.

RODOLPHE. You must. The sun is nearly up. My darling, you know how much I love you, but it's getting too dangerous.

EMMA. I don't care.

RODOLPHE. One day someone will report back to Charles.

EMMA. So be it. Then we'll have no choice but to flee together.

RODOLPHE. No. That would be madness

EMMA. But how else? How else? You do love me?

RODOLPHE. Of course I love you. I adore you.

EMMA (*to* CHARLES). There came a time, I could see, when I was less secure in his love. When perhaps I loved him more than he loved me. But still for both of us it was compulsion, intoxication, madness.

RODOLPHE. Don't think I don't dream too. But you would be finished. You could never come back you'd lose your marriage, your home, your child, everything you know.

EMMA. You are all I want or ever will.

RODOLPHE. It's easy for me. I'm a man, not even married. Free to do as I please. What is not forgiven women, is soon enough forgiven men.

EMMA. I want to declare our love to the world. I so hate this secrecy.

RODOLPHE. I know you do. So do I. But we must be more careful – these early morning rides– you'll be noticed.

EMMA. I'll be more careful. I promise. But I can't do without you. There's Charles' old consulting room: between the cart shed and the stable. Charles has so few patients these days he never bothers with it, but uses the front parlour. I've made it pretty for him.

CHARLES. Between the cart shed and the stable –

EMMA. Understand something. My love for Rodolphe flowed like a tide. Mostly it was full, but sometimes it ebbed away. Then he would seem boorish, ordinary and unromantic. Sometimes I almost dislike him. But he was all I had: I could not bear to lose him. I redoubled my efforts. Wore my prettiest dresses. Changed my hair. Bought him gifts.

RODOLPHE. Emma, I can't take this. It's real silver, and very good silver too. It's too expensive. If I flashed this around everyone would assume I'd come into fortune. Besides, it is Charles who affords this, not you.

EMMA. I am his wife. He endowed me with all his worldly goods upon marriage. Men do, and rightly so, considering how women slave for them. I have power of attorney. I can sign the cheques. I am entitled to run up bills. I know what I can afford. Mr. L'Heureux says what I spend is within my income.

RODOLPHE. What, the draper? How would he know? He is a villain.

EMMA. You must take it, Rodolphe. You must keep it and think of me. It is so beautiful, so delicate. I want you to have it. If you don't take it I'll think you don't love me.

RODOLPHE. Well, put it like that . . .

EMMA. You do love me? Truly love me? Because I love you so much I couldn't exist without you. When I'm not with you, I get angry. I think perhaps you have another woman –

RODOLPHE. Of course I don't have another woman. Good God, where would I find the energy,

EMMA. Don't say that.

RODOLPHE. I love you. I adore you. You know that.

EMMA. I am your servant, your concubine: but you must save
me, Rodolphe. They hate me in this town. Because I am
someone, because I make the best of myself: they talk about
me behind my back. Perhaps they even suspect something.
You must take me away Rodolphe. In Italy people can be
free, can dare to love without shame.

RODOLPHE. Oh poor angel, be brave.

EMMA. Please, please, you must arrange it. You are all the
God I need. Rodolphe, you haven't ever loved anyone else,
have you, like you love me?

RODOLPHE. My dear Emma, I was not exactly a virgin when
you first laid claim to me.

EMMA. I know that with my mind, but not with my heart.
Don't be so cruel.

RODOLPHE. Only you, Emma, Only ever you. I will come
with you to Italy. We will run off together. You will meet me
in the moonlight in the garden. Next time we meet, in this
moonlit garden. I want to be with you forever.

EMMA. But why did my heart feel so heavy? Was I frightened
of the unknown? Did I know even then what was to come?

CHARLES. And then he let you down.

EMMA. No, no. I sent for Mr. L'Heureux.

Enter LHEUREUX

Mr Lheureux, I just have to have a cloak. A lined cloak with
a deep collar. Deep blue I think.

LHEUREUX. To go on a journey, perhaps?

EMMA. No. I just need a cloak. The weather is closing in.
And a new trunk too. Not too heavy: just a nice handling
size. Practical but pretty. You know the kind of thing I like.

LHEUREUX. I know it very well. Such things don't come
cheap

EMMA. Here, take my gold watch, pay yourself out of that.

LHEUREUX. Put it away. It will go on the bill, like everything
else. Good heavens, as if I don't know you and trust you.
Good Lord, if I started worrying now . . .

EMMA. Oh, by the way. No need to leave them at the house. I'll fetch them myself from the shop. A silk lining: a paler blue – oh, you know!

LHEUREUX *smiles a knowing smile and exits.*

RODOLPHE. Emma, we have to put this off a little. Not this coming full moon. Too early. I'm sorry. It will have to wait a week or two. There is so much to arrange.

EMMA. Yes, so much to arrange, for me too. Rodolphe. You do understand that Berthe comes too. We've hardly talked about that. But I can't leave her. A little girl needs her mother.

RODOLPHE. Berthe! Come too?

EMMA. Rodolphe, you look sad, suddenly, and serious. I do understand. Joy can't ever be unalloyed. We are both giving up the life we know. But I'll be everything to you. Your family, your country, I'll look after you, I love you. Don't be sad. And Berthe will turn us into a family.

EMMA. It is true. He let me down. We were to leave on the Monday. I was so happy Charles, so excited. At last my real life was to begin. I waited in the garden in the moonlight for his call. My brave new cloak around me, little Berthe waiting in her room with ribbons in her hair. He did not come. And the next morning I received a letter. A letter. He did not even tell me face to face. He would, he said, always be devoted to me, but if I was leaving, I must leave on my own. It would not be fair to me and Berthe to bring us into this disgrace. 'Teach your child my name,' he said, 'that way you can remember me in your prayers,' and he signed it 'your friend'. My friend.

CHARLES. You expected something different? You were treated like the rubbish you are.

EMMA. I ran across the fields to his house. But he had a visitor. I could hear him talking.

RODOLPHE. I knew she'd be trouble. The best women always are. They start talking about love, making demands. They never understand timing – when things are over. But I must say, Emma Bovary – there's something about her. God, I got as near as dammit to thinking I could be with her for the rest of my life. Intoxicating. But why was she married to such an oaf? He made me think the less of her. But the 'how unhappy I am' approach was clearly going to work. I went to town on that. Then I began to feel sorry for Charles – you know how it is? We men stick together. And you find out what the poor devil has had to put up with. Emma lived like a queen, but he had no money and no patients. Not after l'affaire Hypolite. She wanted to be married to one of France's greatest physicians, not a country bumpkin of a doctor, and he and the pharmacist between them – the greatest bore in all France, by the way – Homais – with Emma egging them on, took a wretched stable boy with a club foot and tried to cure it. They broke all the bones in his foot, hung it with lead weights, and then looked surprised when it went gangrenous. The whole leg had to come off, and the wretched lad only just escaped with his life. That's what happens when men listen to women. And she changed. She started out such a sweet, gentle thing. She became bold, hardened, vulgarised. I suppose that's what deceit does to them. She'd bring me gifts. A gold seal, a cashmere scarf, a silver cigar case – I'd wish she wouldn't. What about poor Charles? If only she hadn't taken it all so seriously. It crossed my mind she might do something silly, hurl herself into the river – but then it would be over, where would be the drama? She'd soon enough find another: there were others before, there'd be others after.

EMMA. I learned my lesson, Charles. I had to bear all that. I was so ill, do you remember? We thought I would die. I could only eat apricots. They grow so well in Italy.

CHARLES. We? What is this 'we' all of a sudden?

EMMA. I turned my full attention back to you. You were every-thing to me. The rock I lent upon. When I was recovered, and was at least able to hold up my head again, face the drabness of my days, I saw Léon for a time, but it was not the same. Compared to Rodolphe he was without substance. Weak, banal in his thoughts, more spiritless than a woman, avaricious, timorous: I looked for reasons to despise him, I don't know why. So that when he too deserted me, I suppose, I could tell myself it didn't matter, I was glad of it.

CHARLES. And still you fucked him. Whenever my back was turned, the pair of you were at it.

EMMA. Don't say it like that. It is all over, in the past. Monsieur Lheureux, of all people, has seen to that.

Mr. LHEUREUX enters.

LHEUREUX. Madame Bovary, it's me. Just a little matter of the bill. We can't let it run up the way it has been. Look here, August third, 200 francs, June 17th, a hundred and fifty: I have a list of goods not paid for, curtains, carpets, a pair of fine slippers, there was that silver cigar box – my, that was a fine purchase, and the cloak was finest batiste, as you specified–

EMMA. You again. How much this time?

LHEUREUX. Two thousand francs. And there's the compound interest at 30 – and my commission on things specially brought in for you from the city.

EMMA. Two thousand? Well, I suppose I must just send out more bills to Charles' patients.

LHEUREUX. I've heard that one before. What patients? My own creditors are closing in Madame Bovary. Perhaps I should approach the good doctor directly?

EMMA. Oh no. Don't do that. Give me just a little time.

LHEUREUX. I could always endorse the bills away. That's to say sell the debt, and leave it to the purchaser to collect the money from you at a later date, plus interest. That could get me out of my own difficulties.

EMMA. I'd rather you didn't do that. It's out of the question.

LHEUREUX. So many things Madame Bovary all of a sudden finds out of the question. She wants what I offer, now, at once, run here, run there, but when it comes to paying, it's a different story. If the endorsee were to go through my books, I suspect we might find it added up to something more like eight thousand francs, than two.

EMMA. That will be all, Monsieur Lheureux. You may go.

CHARLES. He went, but he came back. This letter I wait for is a bill, I take it, a bill I cannot possibly pay. For two thousand, or for eight? It is immaterial. Both are impossible.

EMMA. And this news will affect you, I daresay, more than anything else I have had to say this morning. You've no idea how I have suffered, how I have humiliated myself, how I have tried to save you from this. I love you Charles. You are my husband. My rock, my strength. The rest I cannot help. I turned to Léon for help.

LEON *stands, book in hand. She disturbs his reading and he isn't pleased.*

Léon, please. I don't want to bother you, but I have a favour to ask you. For the sake of what we had together in the past. I need eight thousand francs. You must find it for me. You must save me.

LEON. Emma? Are you out of your mind? How can someone like you owe eight thousand francs?

EMMA. It is money I owe. Charles must not know about it.

LEON. What a great deal does need to be kept from Charles. If it's not one thing it's another. I'm sorry I can't help you, Emma. I don't have that kind of money. You know I don't. That's an enormous amount.

EMMA. You live comfortably. You have things that you could sell.

LEON. Why should I?

EMMA. Because we loved each other.

LEON. I'm sorry. It's just not possible.

EMMA. If you won't do that, then steal it for me. It would be easy. From your employers.

LEON. I'd be sacked. I'd never get another job. I'd be ruined.

EMMA. Love means nothing to you.

LEON. Of course. While one is in it. But it's madness, and it passes. Thank God.

EMMA. I could see it in his eyes. He'd changed – hardened.
The Léon I knew was gone.

LEON. Good Lord, if anything were to put one off marrying, it
would be the terror of ending up with someone like Emma
Bovary. What a wife can get away with, if a man so much
as looks the other way! And this request for money on the
basis of a love affair years in the past? What man would
have any money left at all, if the habit became universal, if
such demands were acceptable? No doubt she'd had other
lovers since; many, I should imagine. I lay awake that night,
I must say. She did seem desperate. I didn't want her to do
anything silly. Suicide is always a possibility. But if she'd
been going to do that, it would have been years back, the
time I told her our meetings had to stop. My mother wanted
me to marry – mainly there was already too much
scandalous talk for comfort. I could see the parting was a
blow to Emma, but what's a man to do? These things wear
out.

EMMA. Mr Lheureux, I implore you, give me time. Don't tell
Charles. I can sell things.

LHEUREUX. You have nothing left to sell.

EMMA. Can't we talk this over?

LHEUREUX. You didn't have much time for conversation in
the past. You were too busy gallivanting. A deep blue cloak
with a paler silk lining to run away in, with your lover. That
came to nothing. We all knew it would. Rodolphe
Boulanger!

EMMA. You knew?

LHEUREUX. The whole town knew. What did you think?

EMMA. Please have mercy, I'll do anything, anything.

LHEUREUX. I believe you would. Anyone would think you
were trying to seduce me. You, the doctor's wife, seduce the
draper to get out of paying a bill. No, I would rather have
my money. Your favours are too cheap for me. In any case it
is too late. I have sold the debt on.

EMMA. You've what?

She turns to go.

LHEUREUX. Don't go, perhaps I was too abrupt, Madame Bovary. Emma. Well, you have gone, and just as well.

EMMA (*to* CHARLES). Last week when you were out the bailiffs came, Charles. They made an inventory. They opened the box I kept my letters in. They laughed and threw them in the fire.

CHARLES. Eight thousand francs. The bill will be for eight thousand francs. I don't have it, nothing like it.

EMMA. I went to Rodolphe for help.

RODOLPHE. My darling Emma. What a surprise! As pretty as ever. The charms stay the same.

EMMA. I don't think so. They have lost confidence. They suffered from your disdain.

RODOLPHE. Don't say that! I never disdained them. We had to part; it was for your own good. What we had was madness. I had to be strong for both of us.

EMMA. Oh yes, all that. It was in your letter.

RODOLPHE. It doesn't mean we couldn't . . . meet perhaps. I have been so unhappy, trying to forget you –

EMMA. Oh yes, all that too.

RODOLPHE. You have someone else, I take it, by now. It was to be expected.

EMMA. No. No. No.

RODOLPHE. Take me back. I've missed you so. Thought of you constantly. Driven myself mad with desire.

EMMA. I need to borrow three thousand francs from you. Eight thousand would be better, but I could stave them off with three. I must have it. I count on your friendship.

RODOLPHE. Friendship? Was that what it was? My dear lady, I don't have three thousand francs to spare.

EMMA. I feel sorry for you. I would have given you everything I had if you came to me. I would have sold all my possessions, worked for you with my hands. I would have begged on the roads for the sake of a smile from you – to know I had eased your pain.

RODOLPHE. I tell you, I haven't got three thousand francs to spare, Emma. Spare me the theatricals.

EMMA *turns to* CHARLES.

CHARLES. What did you expect?

EMMA. I could read his mind. If you love someone enough you can read their mind, did you know that, Charles? The union of souls and minds is so extraordinary-but then one is disappointed: the person at the other end of the love you feel just isn't worthy of it. Disappointment is not a little thing. It's all the difference between life and death. I wanted so much from life and was given so little.

CHARLES. You had everything.

EMMA. You mean I had you, Charles.

CHARLES. I am with simple, good people when they are born and when they die: and I tell you, Emma, compared to them you have everything.

EMMA. But you are at the birth and death of such boring, dull people. It is all you're fit for. If the Marquise de Valleyrois has a baby, you are scarcely going to be there at the birth. Unless it happens by accident, at the roadside, and you happened by.

CHARLES. I hope you die, you are not fit to live. Go on, Emma, take your poison. Cram it into your mouth. Die in agony from arsenic. You will be hideous. Your eyes will pop and strain. Your face will be blotched and distorted. You will scream, You will make noises like the animal you are beneath your silks and finery, your whims and delicacies. Your agony will be ugly. Black bile will dribble from your mouth. I have seen the effects of arsenic. I will watch, and be glad to see you suffer. Others may be sorry for you but not me.

EMMA. Charles, you don't mean this, you're angry.

CHARLES. I mean it.

EMMA. Charles, don't. Oh Charles, come upstairs with me. Let us make this alright again. Forgive me. I am talking about something so long ago. You still love me. Nothing has changed, as you say, except a few words have been spoken over breakfast.

CHARLES. You're indecent.

EMMA. What, to love, in the daylight, while the sun is up – Charles, have you forgotten –

CHARLES. That is all very well for young couples –

EMMA. But I am still young. See, my hands. So white and delicate, as they move against yours. Your strong, powerful hands. Let me make you proud, Charles; your hand here – your warm breath on my neck – kiss me –

She nearly has him. But FELICITE *enters and* CHARLES *disengages himself, returned to his senses.*

FELICITE. The table will have to stay as it is, I see. Un-cleared. I am going to the market, if that suits you, Madame.

EMMA. Yes, Félicité. By all means –

FELICITE *departs.* CHARLES *removes himself from any danger of physical contact with* EMMA.

The day I got the letter from Rodolphe I slapped poor little Berthe, for ruining my life. And I fainted at supper, do you remember, and didn't leave my bed for three months, and still you didn't put two and two together. You decided I had been eating too many apricots; apricots, as everyone knows, contain arsenic. Well, now I will take the arsenic and forget about the apricots. I have it upstairs in our bedroom: I have brought it up from the cellar. The time is nearly ripe.

CHARLES. Your death will not clear my debts. Your death will not pay for the silk slippers and silver cigar boxes you gave your lovers.

EMMA. Mr Lheureux is the thief. He's wicked. He lends at six per cent, takes commission as well, and there's thirty-three and a third per cent on everything he sells. Well, Jesus will forgive me if you won't. Sweet Lord Jesus, who understands everything and forgives everything. He died for our sins. He died for love, as I mean to.

CHARLES. You add blasphemy to your other sins.

EMMA. It is the same love, Charles. It takes a different form, that's all. It is still a sacrament. You understand so little. Honestly, I would rather face the grave than spend the rest of my life with you.

She moves to the piano and plays a bar or two of the Dead March.

You must take no notice of anything I say, darling Charles. I don't want to die; I just don't know what to do. I feel better now I have told you everything. I will be so nice to you now you have no idea. We will live like the birds of the air, upon nothing. You and I, husband and wife, lovers: that is the greatest wealth of all.

CHARLES. Mad.

EMMA. I'm offering you love. I feel free; this great weight is off my mind. You will forgive me because you love me. To think of taking arsenic is absurd. Let's have some more coffee instead. This is quite cold.

CHARLES. What game are you playing now?

She pulls the bell rope.

EMMA. Félicité will have to go; you know she takes advantage of us. I am sure the milk is not today's. I will have to train up a new maid: it is too bad: it is so difficult to find anyone round here with so much as an inkling as to what it is to be a lady's maid.

CHARLES. And how will you pay her wages?

EMMA. Oh, you're so impossibly practical.

FELICITE *appears.*

FELICITE (*ungracious*). Well? What do you want now?

EMMA. You must see what I mean, Charles. Félicité, it is simply not possible to employ you any longer. You will pack your bags and go.

FELICITE. Why?

EMMA. You tell lies and you are dirty. Let me look at your fingernails. They are disgusting. Filthy girl that you are, how can I trust my daughter to your care?

FELICITE. I've been a better mother to her than you ever have.

EMMA. You speak as if you were my friend, not my servant. That is at the heart of my complaint. Bring more coffee first: then go.

FELICITE. Madam, I've used up all the coffee. You told me to. Has she gone mad again, sir?

CHARLES. That's about the size of it.

EMMA. How dare you speak to me like that in front of a servant, Charles. Who do you think you are?

FELICITE. You know who I met down the street just now, madam?

EMMA. Who?

FELICITE. Not one of your gentlemen friends, madam; no sign of them since you started asking round for money. Everyone remarks on it. Poor Mr Lheureux, all he wanted was his money, but you started offering him yourself. Why would he want you? You're not exactly young flesh any more. And think of the hysterics that would go with your embraces. No, he steered well clear of that one.

CHARLES. You heard this, Félicité? In the street?

FELICITE. Oh yes, sir. It's all round the village. She offered herself.

EMMA. I did it for you, Charles.

FELICITE. No, the one I met was that old bitch, the music teacher. Still after her ten thousand francs, for all those lessons you never turned up to once, because you were meeting Mr. Léon. Can't understand that Madame Bovary, she says: what a waste, paying for music lessons and never turning up. I told her you were out. She said she'd heard that often enough: she'd be coming to the door herself if nothing were done.

EMMA. You said I should take piano lessons, Charles. I said we couldn't afford it. You said I must make use of my talents, you so loved to hear me play.

CHARLES. You would play waltzes to me after dinner –

FELICITE. But always with the same old wrong notes that never got any better.

EMMA *changes the tune to a cheerful polka, albeit full of discords.*

EMMA. I am perfect at the piano, perfect. What would I need with lessons? I went to visit Léon, in Rouen. I had to have someone to talk to. His soft hands, his hard lips, his pale bare arms around me. And his voice – it was better than practising scales, Charles, and far more musical.

FELICITE. The lies I told on her behalf, but everyone knew – and how they laughed at you, sir.

EMMA. Léon didn't want his mother upset. It was Léon who brought it to an end, Charles. All women love and lose, I have learned that. But if death were the normal penalty for it, there wouldn't be a woman left alive. This village is full of bitter horrid old women, partly living, because love failed. I will not be one of them: I will not –

FELICITE. All my savings, sir, your wife had all my savings. Now she complains about my nails. Her own hands are filthy sir, filthy. Think where they've been, for all her airs.

EMMA. I sold everything I could until there was only myself left to sell. I offered myself to the notary, so he would not press his bills; it was raining, I went in a wet dress. I lifted my skirt, so, to show my leg – it is such a pretty leg, Charles – and he came towards me, but he was so old and his breath stank and his hand was papery, and I thought of you, Charles, and ran off – and now that is all there is to it, and I am going upstairs to my room, and I will take off the lid of the jar and plunge my hand into it and lift it, and stuff the powder into my mouth, because there is no other escape

for me, none, born in the wrong place at the wrong time;
I cannot live without love, and there is none available in this
world, at least not for me. So I will try somewhere else.
There can be no such thing as extinction. Once dead, I will
at last be alive.

She goes upstairs.

FELICITE. Shouldn't you go after her, sir?

CHARLES. No.

FELICITE *begins to clear the table.* CHARLES *stares into
the fire. A knock at the door.* LESTIBOUDOIS. FELICITE
opens it.

LESTIBOUDOIS. There's another letter. I must have dropped
it. It looks like Mr Lheureux's hand. He's sending out a lot,
these days. Must be in trouble, like so many.

FELICITE. It's the bird of ill omen, back again. Give it to me,
you old black crow; stop cawing and go away. I can't stand
the sight of you.

LESTIBOUDOIS *goes, upset.*

Was this what you were waiting for, sir?

She hands him the letter. CHARLES *shakes his head and
just sits and waits.* FELICITE *tears up the letter and throws
it in the fire, leans against the mantelpiece and waits as well.*

End.